Of Swans and Stars

FINDING MY OWN NORTH STAR, ONE POEM AT A TIME

E. M. McConnell

Of Swans and Stars: Finding My North Star, One Poem at a Time

Copyright © 2022 by Eryn McConnell

Pubishing and Design Services by MelindaMartin.me

ISBN: 978-3-00-072595-1

For my bird, my butterfly and my bee.

Without you there would be

no magic, no love, and no hope.

Contents

On Being Hopeful

Of Swans.................................... 3

Of Stars...................................... 4

The Music Calls......................... 6

The Storytellers......................... 8

Hear the Hoofbeats 10

Music 11

Couch Lily 12

Lockdown 13

Scars 14

Facing the Brave 16

Of Love

I See 19

What If It Is?............................... 20

Will You?..................................... 22

What about It, King?.............. 25

Colonising Hearts.................... 28

She Said 30

Father 32

Walls 34

Her Roses 36

He Said.. 39

This Is What It's About........... 40

A Man of Many Flavours 42

The Lighthouse Shines
for Me..................................... 44

On Being Hopeless

Lockdown Rage 49

November 19 50

On Writing, Yet 52

A Sewing Repair
   for the Soul 54

Prison Bars into Wind 56

Blind Passengers 58

Detox 60

I Remember 62

Dark 63

He's the One 64

Hallways at 21 66

O, My Muse! 68

The Game Starts Again 69

Shadow Face 72

Clarity 74

Of Myth and Magic

Samhain 79

Sunset in a Cornfield 80

Mabon 82

Samhain Eve 84

The Sea Dragons 86

Dragons in Myth 88

Darkest Night 91

Saint George and a Dragon .. 92

Can They? 94

The North Wind 96

The East Wind 98

The South Wind 100

The West Wind 102

Fire 105

Selkie 108

Maze 110

The Raven Call 112

Acknowledgements 115

About the Author 117

On Being Hopeful

Of Swans

I look out and behold there
The swans, a symbol of my home
Growing slow and seeing small
Those white wings framed in black
Head held high in regal pride
Holding firm their Queen's promise;
The protected birds of the Crown.
They sing to me of Manannan and Lir
Their loyalty and courage strong
They would not be subsumed
They would not disappear into dark
Falling slow into oblivion.
O to be a swan.
If I could spread my wide wings
And fly so far away
Reaching for the pale moon
With my light against the night
Finding my way home.

Of Stars

The heroes live in the sky
Blazing bright at night
The blackened sable a foil
Their lines emblazoned true
To be seen by eyes far and wide
The Sickle, Caster, Orion
The North Star, he so certain
Guiding us home, always.
The stars call to those
Who cannot find their way
Seeking so blindly here and there
Hands grasping at sand and air
Looking for a rope, to hold
They sing out so clear, so true
Wanderer, hear us, for we are here.
The heroes there in the sky
Placed there by feckless Gods
For us to remember their glory
They call out still to us
To bring us home, to the stars.
O to be a star. I could fly high
I could see the world from afar
And remember anew the beauty

Setting aside the sorrow, the pain.

I could sit with the heroes of old

Place myself in a constellation

In a corner of the Great Plough

I could seek and sing and shine

Being part of something more

Than just myself, of my flesh.

I could fly my way home…

Looking up to the North Star

I hear the echo slowly sing

Follow me, find me, child

Find your way slowly home.

The Music Calls

The music weaves again so slowly

And melancholy stretches a finger

Guided by a plaintive cello note

Aimed directly at my blistered soul

As I wait, poised between paused sound

And then I am trapped within the staves

As the music unfolds its sweet tapestry

And I understand, O I understand so ...

How it was and how it can be again

The universe ignites a series of sparks

And my visual landscape follows suit

Creating notes to walk on as I learn

And I see the pattern of golden thread

Shimmer in its endless swaying dance

Motion in my frame is stilled sudden

To match the seeing within

And my mind begins to wrap around

The melody that continues to call

My heart yearns to understand the strings

Oh if I could be one with the world so

To be free to fly and climb up so high

To strike a resonant melody into amber

Holding it safe in my hesitant hands

And seeing it solidify into hard gem
The wishes running warm in my veins
And pouring out of my open eyes
It holds a whispered promise sent
As yet unfulfilled but created still
Of something else, another road
A journey in glimmering light
Which falls drop by drop into my mind
And my fingers hum and twitch to reach
To trace the lines and pattern in the air
To caress the hope that resonates there
And catch the promise flowing to my hand.
The melody fades into expectant dusk
And I stand transfixed with understanding
My mind alight with possibilities
The song will always end in our ears
But it goes on, unrepentantly
Within our dreaming souls.

The Storytellers

Once upon a time, all the tales say

As they touch gently on hero and foe

Bravery and honour and swords and woe

And then we close the book and sigh

Leaving the great stories behind us

Or so they say.

Storytellers do not just live in books

Noses tweaked within forgotten pages

And hands twitching at book spines

As we leave them to moulder on shelves

In decaying dusty houses of paper.

You can see storytellers in the stars

Haunting tales of Greek heroes of old

Who foiled the Gods and their plans

And when they breathed a last breath

Instead of a hoped for quiet peace

They became fire in a midnight sky.

You can hear storytellers in the rain

An endless turning cycle of water

Travelling between the heavens and earth

Carrying with it a flood of stories to tell.

You can feel storytellers in the hearth

Warming your face as dark coals burn

And towers alight and temples groan
As they stumble and crumble to ash.
We too are storytellers it is truth
And we are tethered tight to the story
That we all must tell
Pulled here and there by taut thread
Dancing ever like sentient marionettes
But pull again we must and patiently
We stop to tease and unravel the thread
Our thread, which links us to so many stars
And as we pull all the threads start to sing
Forming an unearthly harmony within
And we see the old tales form again
In the dusty books, up in the bright stars,
In the shining rain and in our own hearts.

Hear the Hoofbeats

If you hear the hoofbeats, follow them

Set your compass and chase the spark

Find what sets your soul alight, dear one

Never cease; till your soul settles in a daze

Hearken to the hoofbeats in your blood

To that new and dangerous rhythm

Lest one day it should silence

And you are adrift without a guide.

Music

The beat skips and slithers down the cord

Dodging errant quavers with amusing grace

And it reaches into my expectant ears

Pulling my soul out of myself, flying free

To abandon my precarious grounding

My feet lift and leave the soundless earth

My soul singing in joy as it tastes freedom

Neurons fire, mis-fire and realign seamlessly

And my heart soars high within the resonance

Of a beautiful, perfectly formed lyric

Hovering gently around jagged emotions

And soothing the edges with velvety tone

Anaesthetising with a well placed guitar solo

That sashays ever closer, vibrating higher

With an intoxicating understanding within

I hear you, it whispers and I see you too

This, this cacophony of feeling, I hear it

Encapsulation of mundane angst and fear

In just one perfect fucking song line

And I want to take that wordsmithery

And preserve it in warm clear amber

So it stays forever true, in my heart

That day, long ago, that song, right there

It saw me. It saw all of me.

Couch Lily

I sit and I think and I dream

As to act is just too fiery

I am a lily and I like to sit

In a watery spot to dream

Life is prettiest here.

But I sit and I remain

Floating like a couch lily

Aimlessly dreaming

Through entropy and decay

Never forming and growing

Just dreaming endlessly

But it's just so pretty here.

Why don't you sit here a while?

Abide with me and dream

See what you see with me

And float away in the wave

Decay doesn't touch the lilies

We are too beautiful to die

So we float and we dream

And slowly we fade away

Seeping into a wave

But oh so aesthetically.

Lockdown

People wear masks nowadays.

A gentle cacophony of colour; red, green, gingham.

It's soothing against the grey.

I like it.

People smile with their eyes these days.

Corners crinkling furiously, eyes sending love, heartbeams.

I love that.

People bow, wave and nod these days.

Hands are forbidden, unclean.

People reach out with laser beams of courtesy,

I see you, we are here.

I like it.

People stop and look at things these days.

Raindrops on leaves, birds nesting, kids jumping in puddles.

Our eyes eat it up like we're starving wolves.

I love that. We need that.

Corona is a canny virus but we can adapt around it,

make our lives around it.

We are a better, stronger virus;

thanks again for the wisdom, Agent Smith.

When it's kicked to the kerb,

Can we keep the nice things?

Scars

How do you wear your scars, she asked
Gently touching her palm to the spot
Silvered light snaking its way to my soul
That small hint left of unimaginable pain
Buried deep under layers of defence.
I looked at her in surprise, so unsure
How do I wear these? As everyone does.
I hide them away, so nobody sees
I keep them in the shadow far away.
But yet people see them still, said she.
So why do you hide them away
As if you are ashamed of your life
Those are your own marks, to show
How you climbed slowly up and out
Of driving away the horror long ago
Why do you not wear them?
How could I wear these though?
To bear them on my face, stark gold
Bold stripes of rage snarling there
To drive people away, set me apart
As a warrior in life, grim and strong?
Or should I emblazon them here
Nestling in my palms within lines
So when I crumple my hand shut
I can feel the pain anew in faint echo

Would then those who take my hand
See those marks and know me well?
Or perhaps I should brand them there
Away from my face, high on shoulders
Right where my wings could have been
The scars that ripped away my wings to fly
That kept me grounded, afraid to fall
The scars that bound me to earth.
Where should I wear them then? I plead.
Instead of wrapped in dark and shame
How can I release them, blinking into light
Ready to stand as memory of what was
But never will be again, I know
How can I do this?
She looked and smiled gently at me
Her eyes shining like pools of rain
Do just that, dear one, whispered she
Bring them out into the light with grace
And let them settle where they will
Wear your scars with open pride,
Be they as warrior grim and strong
Or healer, reaching to those who fall
Or as wisdom teller guiding slow
Those who still hide in fear and dark
Wear them just where they fall.
Bear them gently with your pride.
Wear your streaks of silvered flame.

Facing the Fear

We all know fear by now
The familiarising of cold
That starts as the blood cools
But at some point then the fear
Bends to something else, a promise
That now we can be brave.
Sometimes the fog clears slow
And our heart galvanises strength
Bringing hot rage to cool and reform
And we stand, strong, healing
Hearing our courage sing low
That this love is our song.

On Love

I See

What do I see?

I see eyes framed in green and gold

Soft heart brimming in bright glass

A limpid expression, open and warm

This is what I see.

I see a face etched with strong bone

Holding safe a gently curving mouth

My hands flitting out, wanting to touch

And draw the line of your smile

This is what I see.

What do I hear?

I hear a laugh that rides free

Scattering light like summer rain

Wrapping itself around my mind

And pulling me effortlessly in

This is what I hear.

I hear a warm voice musing in delight

That listens and hears, understands

Uttering living words of raw poetry

Wrapped in gold bonds of honour

And true refreshing honesty.

This is what I hear.

What if It Is?

They say love is an intractable force

A rushing river that forces you away

But I wonder, over and over, if that is so

Because love is not running away, but stop.

You heard me well, I said love is stop.

Pressing blindly through a sea of faces

For just one who looks and sees and nods

Who understands how you sing life's song

Or travelling with feet in a green blur

Tasting and touching upon countries

Like they are merely building blocks

That can be switched and exchanged

But our feet never look and actually see

Love is not to keep running onward

But to stop. To say, I do not know yet

If life is not Fate but Serendipity merely

But this is enough. I stop, for this.

Love is stop. No more forcing to fit

And pushing gasping through hurdles

Ignoring where your limits still lie

In the endless race to move onwards

It's stopping to listen and look and smile

And being kind to those who run on

It's bidding farewell to those who fly

Soaring in the sky, blind to those who fall

Love is saying, this is enough, I AM enough

No more frenzy of moving endlessly

No forced action that runs yet in place

Stop means still grow, but yet curiously.

Stop means turning from helpless dream

Faded colour bright in its memory

Seeing the right direction spark bright

And your soul answers affirmatively.

No more frenzied run on neon roads

Or desperate flight into white clouds

It's turning apace, slow and calm

And reaching to your own soul

Hand outstretched and open

Saying, this is enough. We are home.

Will You

Will you swim with me?

Let's find a deep blue ocean

Inviting, adventurous and warm

Lets dive, surf and laugh

Our best parts meeting each other

Radiant souls resonating.

I see you. You see me. Let's be.

No need to go anywhere, lets swim

And bask and splash under the Sun.

Will you build a boat with me?

It doesn't need to be large,

Just something built for two.

Fixtures gleaming, new paint smiling

The laughing dreams of high ambitions

Big plans and bigger ideals

To speed us over the ocean.

Let's make waves and let the wind

Tangle our hair as we fly into the Sun.

Will you find an island with me?

As our feet begin to still

And the boat grows small

Shall we find a spot, a new place to roam?

A warm island please, with plenty to grow

Prosperous soil and mountains, a valley

So we can weather the storms and the cold.

Will you build a castle with me?

We've done all our swimming

Paddling in the ocean, showing our best

Selves like fresh-pressed suits

And clear sparkly eyes

Let's turn our thoughts to building something.

Will you build it with me?

I can fashion a castle, courtly and fine,

Insubstantial and towering, like drops of rain.

But to build I need hands, an extra heart.

Let's use bricks and beams

Of our values, our hopes.

I shall bring honour, and hope and strength

A spark of tenacity, a gritted tooth.

Can you bring some patience and a recipe book?

We will need floors of compassion,

Pillars of time

Doors of humility and stairs to climb

Windows to look out of, for when we can't see

And some sparks of clarity,

Perhaps this you can carry.

Will you drift away with me?

I am old now, and tired – my hands

Are worn and gnarled. I can build a raft

Simple and light – but I would like a blanket

To hold me tight. For warmth.

I am tired now. I have no need to dream

I want to close my eyes and drift

In the endless, loving Sea.

I can give back all the echoes

Of my life

And warm the hopes

Of the swimmers that I can see.

And maybe one day as the Sun sets low

And the pink in the sky speckles and glows

I will open my eyes and there you will be

Saying, come, love. Come drift with me.

What about It, King?

So you want to be King in my story
Will you wear your golden crown
On top of your head at a jaunty angle
Like you won the fucking lottery?
And what chapter of this story
Are you after then, O hopeful King?
This chapter, the acknowledgements
In a sparkling new illustrated edition
Or maybe you want the happy ending?
And what will you do to earn this, O King?
Will you fight all the famed dragons
With fiery maw and poisoned claw
Will you gallop in with armour new
And blazing sword bright a-waving?
Or did you plan to swagger on by
Waving your Netflix subscription
A cheeky lustful come to bed grin
And a worn takeaway menu in hand?
So you want to know who I am -
Well that's a difficult one really
O hopeful applicant King
Because in this tale of mine
I am merely a flawed narrator

Who is still fathoming what I am
So really you, O crowned one
Will be the last to know who I am.
But when I find out, I'll tell you.
So you want me to sing to you softly -
Oh well, O King of my story
That could be difficult really
As my voice is not sweet and pure
It does not summon birds and
Tantalising butterflies to my hand
It is rasping and ragged and strong
And thoughtless and sometimes wrong
And I would not sing, to you, O King.
What will you bring to my story, King?
Will you seek honour and rich hope
And bring warm humour to the pages
Of my sometimes melancholy tale?
How will you enrich this blank page
That you wish to improve so softly?
Are your pages strong and vividly
Painted with battles conquered within
And learning and loving and tears
That tells the wandering tale
Of a humble, strong yet noble man
Who wanders his life seeking to live

Crownless perhaps, but still proud

With something worthy to add here

Next to my flawed and worthy script?

A book and a tale is good enough

With its flaws and turns and dead ends

It needs no King or Queen or Prince

To make it great, to make it real

A book needs no crown to grace it

Its beauty lies in the telling of it.

But put aside your tarnished crown

And set your feet to walking a chapter

Alongside me - and maybe we'll see.

Colonising Hearts

Do you remember

Colonising my heart?

Changing the rooms about

To suit your fickle fancy

Just improving the look

But now I can't put it back

The old spaces have shrunk

Back into indistinct lines

You took over and I let you

And now I can't put it back

To how it was. To how I was.

You promised to cauterise

My silvered opened scars

And I can't feel them now

My marks of bitter survival

Have silvered and smoothed

Burnt away so cleanly

But wait I needed those -

They were my road map

Of where I have been

And not to go again

You flame proofed my skin

And held me so tenderly

To let your love renew me

But now I can't feel it

That cool enquiring breeze

And my fire can't warm me

I am sanitised and purified

An identikit clean fortress

You gave me your grace

Your gift of love

Even though you left

It is home to me

Because I am changed

Cells, blood and genes

And now here I must stay

Where you colonised me.

She Said

She said she cries too much
That's what they always told her
As tears welled up like raindrops
At the first sign of joy or pain
She feels like a moving river
Rushing and flowing endlessly
But the tears sing as they cleanse
And she can feel again, clearly.
She sees in feelings and emotions
And in everything she can feel
She moves like an ever moving river
Swimming through cycles of feeling
Changeable and deep and strong
I wish I could feel like you do, she said.
She said she doesn't feel anything
That's what they always told her
A barren and deserted terrain
Where the soul retreats from pain
She feels like a mountain range
High up and solid and strong
But the rain cannot reach here
Up aloft in the static clouds
She carries her pain, but remotely

With no risk of it washing away.

She sees in information and fact

And in everything she can see

She moves like a dark hurricane

Swirling inwards to a dead still sea.

I wish I could feel like you do, she said.

Father

Sometimes I catch a glimpse

Of a tawny eye, with a wry smile

And I want to rush over

With a thousand questions

Did I get it right? Do you miss us?

Are you happy -

And then your eye shifts to

Be a warm-eyed stranger

And I turn away.

Sometimes when the west wind moves

And I smell the waft of cool moors

I can hear your laugh dancing in the air

The timbre of your voice like rain

And I strain to hear, to catch -

And the wind slips away.

Sometimes when I sing at night

I hear your shadow, singing too

The crescendo of mingled voice

And then it fades to a resonance

Just my echo

I keep your tobacco stained fingers

And your warm laugh

And your head held high

Your spark of joy

I carry them wrapped in a west wind

In the sparkle of a hazel eye

In the shadow of a song

In our hearts.

I start the story with

Once upon a time

There was a man

A strong and flawed man

And we keep him safe and whole

In our hearts

In our songs

In our clasped hands

We won't forget

Walls

The clouds roll in slow, steel grey and cold
And I see the storm reflecting in your eyes
I see your need to find a reason to live
Clutching at the table with whitened knuckles
Trying to scrabble and find something real
As your indecision draws and pulls you down
I watch you stumble and career in your life
From walls and broken fortress, abandoning
Your safe boltholes and running through rage
Wounds gaping open and fractures keening
And I see you pause and gasping, looking up
At that grey, grey sky. At the clouds so cold.
I am an invisible figure standing at the end
Of your life road, waiting for you to find me.
But I am not just here to take you away
Willing you through the fabric of time
I am here as your ancient cornerstone
And I can build a stone fortress, just for you.
I can wrap walls up around your fear
I can build empty rooms to house your pain
Dark windows to walk behind in sorrow
And gleaming dark floors to lie in repose
Walls. I can give you walls. Walls of time.

You are more than a reflection of the sky

You are more than your deeds and pain

You are more than the whispers in your soul

A sum of parts, adding your Fate to mine

I look on you, watching your journey onward

Drawing inexorably closer to me. To the end

And I am drawn too to your flicker of light

The hope driving you on, the heart-shine

I will hold on to the stars in those eyes

Because it is my glimpse into your world

And I sit and I look and I crave your light

So I shall build walls for you, dark and strong

I'll be your cornerstone, waiting for you

Because you are more than the world to me

You are the journey and my destination.

I sit and I wait for you at World's End.

Her Roses

I think on flowers idly, as I must

For I write of dragons and flowers

And so many species jump to mind

But then one shoulders its way up

Bullishly, claiming its space in style

The thorned and green stemmed Star

Ringed with her proud, pouting petals.

The Rose. It's always, always the rose.

But is a rose really then a dragon?

We know thanks to the great Bard

That a rose by any other name smells

Just as sweet - as a Capulet -

Could it be in truth called a cabbage

And still have its charismatic allure?

Even then, simpering sweet as it is

It is still not a dragon. How could it be?

A flower is soft and sweet and frail

A dragon is strong and dark in dignity

But my muse guides me quietly

And I see her, as she was long ago

Bent in a garden of blooming flowers

With green gloves and tools in hand

Cutting the roses that she so loved

And she turns to smile so crookedly

I look on with longing and sorrow

At this figure beckoning me in

But she's not a dragon! I cry.

She was merely a woman, but mine

A woman who loved and tended

And fought for me so bravely

But yet bone and flesh and heart.

She is no dragon, I said.

Look within and further, says a voice

And obeying I look and look at her

And I see a woman, a small body

But within, her courage bursts out

In bright flame and fired light

Her sinews lie under her soft skin

Her wings stay curled into her back

She softened her eyes from molten gold

And her hands crept into soft fingers

Covering her twisting iron claw

Her heart remained, as a dragon

Her courage red hot and furious

Her dignity stayed, as a dragon

Holding her head up through ages

And I look and my heart fractures

Into infinitesimal small pieces

If she was a dragon, she would be here

Dragons stay and dragons live

Flying high and strong and true

But the flowers beckon me again

Gesturing with velvet soft petals

But I did live, they murmur low

I live on in my treasure, my loves

In my red roses, child, and in you.

He Said

He said; we fit together, you and I

I want to be the amber to your dragonfly

Unchanging, unmoving in beauty

So I can worship you, you see

He said, you fit to me, my best part

Like the ever missing jigsaw piece

Rushing home to a joyous feast

You belong here, you've found your home

Never more do you always need to roam

Rest here, be safe,

Be the lady to my Lord

Let me entwine you, Love,

In tender silken cord

We belong together, you know,

Always, you and I

So quietly did the spider croon,

To his captured fly.

This is What It's About

It's not about the curve of your eye

Or the sweep of your eyelash on

A perfect cheekbone

It's about the promise that shines

In your eye

To keep my secrets safe

And shoulder my tears and my years

When my arms and heart are weak.

It's not about the timbre of your laugh

And the tone of your voice

Rich and strong and sweet

It's about the promises you utter

And keep, over and again

With, I love you. We made this together

And I am here.

It's not about the dance of bone

Gracefully splayed in your hand

Knuckles dusted with work

And hands holding strength

It's about those hands keeping

The chores and the stones

Upright and strong

In our shared life and joys

Honouring and building our life.
It's not about a white picket fence
And bright white curtains gleaming
In the perfect dream house
It's about promises that never break
And a shared private glance
And wide shoulders to carry
And hands to hold me when I fall.
It's the honour in your heart
And wisdom in your eye
And patience in your hand.
It's about marriage and love
And determination and hope
And knowing that you
Will build something with me
And stand to protect it
Against the winds of time
And the sands of life
Until we both fall into dust
This is what it's about.

A Man of Many Flavours

I am a man of many flavours, said He
With quizzical smile flowing freely
But truth is ever told with jest they say
And I saw truth lurking behind the smile.

You are indeed a man of many flavours
And you will have to forgive the extra 'u'
Replied I; but should I count the ways?
Maybe Shakespeare of old, with pen true
Discharged that phrase more delicately.

I do certainly see many flavours in you
Shifting within mercurial, colourful moods
Hiding their radiance in deep lilac shadow
But oftimes blazing joyful in bright sun.

Vinegar be the first, that is certainly true.
But not a dark malt, humble and strong
Maybe you are more like a moody balsamico.

A smooth appear with a peppered edge
Setting people off balance with practiced charm
Then a bite as a warning when you depart
Their eyes streaming at the crisp tartness.

Yes love, your flavour is this.
But then of course the tone shifts and moves
Becoming the warm laugh of a ruby wine

A fragrant nose with a full bodied taste

And a lingering hearty forest of fruit

Like a perpetual golden autumn in haze.

This is you, too, love, you must admit.

But under this is another layer yet, so hid

Warm and sweet with sunburnt caramel

Not so peppered and caustic yet

Still with a heady mix of smoke and rain.

A sweet and strong lingering on the tongue

A temperate autumn singing its last song

Yes, love, your flavour is certainly this.

And then? I know not. But perhaps one day

I will see.

The Lighthouse Shines for Me

I shine a light for you my love

And for you only will I shine

I hope that you always see it

Even as you sleep and rest deep.

The light I shine is warm and strong

To guide you home while I am gone

I watch over you while I am far away

And my heart pines for you, always.

I stand alone in the deep dark

So so far away from you, love

While the sun shines out strong

Over fields of green for you.

An entire ocean separates us

And countless birds flying between

You are too far for me to reach

And to touch your face

But I shine my light for you, love.

You shine a light for me, too,

I know, and you built a tower

So graceful, tall and strong

The light shines out gold in certainty

And you watch over me too

You keep my soul safe and warm

While I sleep and sometimes dream.
I walk in my dreams alone and cold
Wishing for you to be near me
But I feel the light shining out again
And I know you are there still
I hear your words in my memory
Your promises that you keep
I know, love, that you care.
You are everything to me love
And always, always will be
Even though you are so far.
One day the water will no more
Separate us so completely
And we will not need the lights
To guide our way home.
But until then I will shine my light
So hopeful and strong in gold
And look out over the dark sea
To watch over my beloved
And keep my promise told.
When I see your tower of light
Smiling gently back at me
Blazing sharp over the dark sea
I will know you are there love
And there you will forever be.

On Being Hopeless

Lockdown Rage

Bleib gesund, stay inside

Halt abstand, stay alive

Sparkly neon chatty lines

Snappy soundbites

Directions to herd us

This way and that.

I saw the woman, white mask bedecked

I saw the sanitary bubble

Spilling around her like

Congealed dark ink.

Fear marks her out.

Gravitate and magnetise

Using our orbits to keep away

Our hands starved of blood

But ever the neon soundbites

Feed us intravenously.

Blieb. Immer. Gesund.

Halt. Abstand.

November 19

The news blares out loud
Sharp flickers of voice in sound
Where one country leads first
Another always follows after.
It's coming for us too.
The murmurs start to roll and hum
The old word resurfaces on lips
Lockdown is coming back they say
They tighten their masks fearfully
And people look askance at others
Looking for the branded unclean.
Who do we blame and fear now?
The walls start to close back in
And faint hope of reunion slips away
Quietly into the night it flees
Away from my once hopeful hands.
I am not ready to be shut in the dark
With the walls closing in slow
Hearing tinned promises from lying face
This will be over soon, they say.
It's for your own good, they say.
But they know they're lying too.
Shops will shutter away silently

Schools will hide behind app screens
And books will shut with a slam.
The doors will close with a click.
My world shrinks around me slow
Tightening as an ever eager noose
The walls. The walls are coming.
I do not believe anymore or then
When they say it will just be weeks
An emergency stop measure
This time when the walls close
We will not come out again.
They have taken their power gladly
To imprison a nation on a whim
And they close the doors smiling
Believing they are doing good.
But the walls do not care
If it is a good reason or not.
When the walls close this time
We will not be the same again.
When the walls close this time
We may not wish to leave again.

On Writing, Yet …

My pen calls to me again

Like a shivering cool wind

Rattled in the corner of my mind

A gentle shake that climbs

From the corners of my memory

And an idea unfolds and flutters

But oh so feebly yet

Taking flight uncertainly

A fragment of a beautiful line

Emerges on the white page

Like a negative pooling on film

But I do not know how to write it

To finish it, to bring it to its glory

So I hold it so gently in my palm

Cradling it from the elements

In the hope that it will gasp and live

And grow, stretching out its wings

Growing into glorious flight

My thoughts scratch like birds

Clamouring to be released to the air

Their delicate wings thrashing

And their warm feathered breasts

Opening to gasp the new breath

But my pen cannot paint them

Quickly enough to capture it

To show their transient beauty

And their wings flutter and fade

Even while my pen commands me

To write it, just write it, now!

And my hand spills confused ink

As my fingers flex and flow

But the sound keeps eluding me

Dancing just out of my grasp

And I am left with cold silence

And a mourning empty in my heart

That I couldn't sing their song.

The verse retreats into the deep

And my pen slows and rests

Glowering reproachfully at

Its muted owner who slumps

With dejected, furrowed brow

Heart spent with empty hands.

A Sewing Repair for the Soul

The light dims and slows around

As I sit and think with face stilled

And I realise that I have lost time

Seconds and minutes flowing by

She slipped past me furtively

My eyes open wide but unseeing.

My mind fumbles helplessly

At a loss to handle the dull pain

Inspecting it so gingerly, fearful,

As if it is really a wild animal

Crouching there, cornered,

Ready to bite.

And I do not know what to do

As each of my shadows shouts out

Calling for a different way, a new plan

But all clamour for the same command

Run. Run far away. Get away. Be free.

I scramble back to myself hastily

Pulling together rent edges of composure

Hearing my seams rip and tear in edge

Threads flailing and tissue gaping

And I hear feet thundering in my head

It is time. It's time to go. Run.

I need to hibernate as an animal
Who is wounded deep in its nest
Alone and high in the pale winter sun
I need to hear only peace and silence.
And I need to forget.

Prison Bars into Wind

Grey they are and solid, glinting

So softly in the pale sunlight

They are ever present in our gaze

A reminder of where you were

And where you still are

And where you cannot go

Until time turns slowly again.

They are our walls that keep us in

They keep us crouching so small

They are the blows that rain down

They are the sneer that ever

Cuts your soul into pieces

The hand that dissects thread by thread

Until you know no more who you are

They are our pain, our memories scored

So deep and dark on our scarred hearts

And we hold on to our prison bars

We beg to be released from them yet

We still hold on to them so desperately

What if our prison bars turned to wind

And we are left gaping at clean air

Precious opportunity shining in our hands

As we step out from our prisons into light

I know my prison bars still yet remain

They are branded within a broken soul

Where I dare not believe there is more

Looking at something gleaming bright

A promise of a dream unlooked for

I know not if I can reach out for it

Or if as my hand touches that dream

It will fester and darken in decay.

But I wish for those prison bars to fade

And maybe that is enough.

But then, as the prison bars dissipate

And dissolve away into a cool wind

What then? What then? What of you?

Will you hold onto that past

Clamouring in nostalgic despair?

Will you mourn your captivity lost

Fearing your new uncertain future?

Or will you step out into the light

And leave the bars far behind?

Blind Passengers

We open our eyes but we cannot see

We move among people bewildered

We reach with our hands to touch

But keep missing those who reach

Who are trying to find us

Sitting on the bus so crowded

Fingertips stretch out to a window

And raindrops creep, caressing

We crave the connection

But cannot see the crowd around

Who cannot see us

We are the blind passengers

Stowed away without a raft

Looking out for the next wave

That could rush in, devouring

But wishing to simply fly

High and far away

Sometimes we say we know

Where our journey will end

Clutching our road map tightly

And greedily to our chest.

But the dark sea wrenches it

Hurling it far away

And we flail, helplessly.

Never will you have a road map

You are a blind passenger here

Feeling the roads in the dark

Tripping this way and that

Hand outstretched for your guide

But the wind rips them away

We are blind passengers here

Reaching out to find a warm heart

But they want saving too

And your hands flounder

And slip away. Emptily.

The sea surrounds us now

And we stagger aimlessly

The waves push and shape us

Moulding us to the dark swell

Floundering and gasping

As we submit to the tide

We are blind passengers

Even when we think we see

We are alone in a sea of people

Just drifting around

Live flotsam and jetsam

Seeking so blindly.

Detox

I did everything to forget you
Following the instructions
On the tin precisely, you know
I poured the salt at the door
I burned sage to clean and purify
I even dissected my heart a little
Just removing the sore parts
And I reminded myself, often
This is me evolving. Evolving pain.
But I felt a splinter of you remain
Hiding just underneath my skin
It won't hurt to yank you out
But the memory of you might
When it surfaces like a wave
Seeing you laugh so deeply
When you opened your soul
Loving and leaving is merely
Part of life's great journey
And we grow, evolve and revolve
Spinning and oscillating darkly
Into a newer, better frequency
And we leave those childish ideals
Far behind like crumpled clothes

Deserted, an elusive afterthought.
But sometimes a part betrays us
Like a plaintive call deep within
A slow quiet keen of mourning
A wish for something to be again
Our treacherous echo of heart
Our wishing for another time
Another chance, of another life
You may not be good for me
On that my soul and heart agree
But you were sweet and wholesome
And somehow you dissolved quickly
Into my jaded, hardened skin
And there you stayed, a splinter
And I am not ready, quite ready
To exorcise you. But I must forget you.

I Remember

I remember the day

Frozen in the view of mountains

and Staind on the radio

Frenzied electronic denials flying

Voices across the world denying

But no, not really? How could he?

Someone larger than life can beat death

Just stop the world, they said.

But we can't get off. You know that too.

I heard the shriek of tyres

Repeated in my dreams

And the murmuring voices

Reassuring you to sleep

I heard you when you visited

To say it would be OK

That you loved me once

I remember the day

When everything changed.

Dark

Darkness grows like spilled ink

Quietly it spreads out, and seeping

An inevitable spread of territory

Outward. Reaching.

Rippling over unsuspecting land

Dark swarms like an insect horde

with a purposeful hum

Moving this way, that way,

Seeking. Ever focused.

The dark, sings, sweetly, of the dark.

A numbing anaesthetic

No more feeling, as we fall back

Into night. Into the rushing silence.

Our screaming edges stilled and…

Everything slows.

We caress the numbing thought

Edges are smoothed

Why go back to the light? It calms us.

In the dark we understand.

Abide in the still and the slow drip.

The dark spreads slowly.

Outward like a stain.

Where it conquers, it stays.

He's the One

Sunlight flows as the front door opens
And she joyfully ushers a new face in
Her heart opening and loving bright
With matrimonial hopes blooming anew
And in her eyes sits the plea to us
Don't ruin this for me. He's the one.
We nod and smile, in our Sunday best
And we mind our manners and sit well
Looking on the new man in our lives
And we hope that he really is the One
So she will be happy. So she stays happy.
And then as the love starts to sour
And his fists fall on our faces like rain
We are the ballast between them
The barrier to a perfect true love
And swollen eye shut looks in fear
On a cold shuttered face so grim
As she spits from an angry mouth
You always spoil it, you're like him
And the man disappears from view
While she keens and wails again
Her hopes put back in a dark box
Waiting for the next new face

To be ushered in the front door

With beaming face and heart

And a quiet whispered wish to us

Don't ruin this for me. He's the One.

Hallways at 21

A black and white print framed in red

A man somberly holding his baby

A trite, oversold and over-seen trope

But it stays in my memory still

As it crouches in a dark hallway

I remember hard fists raining down

In a desperate, fierce rhythm

And my face burned in response

There is a beauty in that kind of rage

As it decimates your face and spirit

My head drummed against that print

I knew its sound intimately

And then you stopped to pause

After hitting me interminably

Perhaps to inspect your handiwork

Oh so dispassionately.

I find myself visiting that print

See the fists fall in dangerous dance

And my cheekbones flare and scream

But my mouth stays silent, always.

My mouth always did love you

In traitorous curves and edges

Do you ever visit that dark hallway?

Do you regret your nearly killing me?
Or does that memory conjure warmth
And a dark joy when you remember?
My cheekbones still remember
As I look again on that trite print.

O, My Muse!

Just write, if you need to

Murmurs my muse.

A light shines the way on my page

Words tumble, frantically.

Just write, when you pick up

The pen, admonished He.

Write, for me, like a dance of love

Spin, bend and turn, maniacally.

Just write, if you need to cry

Gently whispered he.

Salt wet tears fill a paper boat

To sail the trembling words away.

Just write, sang my muse

As he climbed the tower of words

And plucked out my gasping heart

While smilingly turning away.

Just write, echoes my Muse

Small fragmented sounds

Hardly reaching my ear

I grasp and fumble for my page

To see it slowly flutter away.

The Game Starts Again

The Game started swiftly with drama

As it always did then, with a start

A searing flash of feral intent

Sliding into his eye as he shifted

Into his predator skin. Ready for rage.

His humanity left shamefacedly

Leaving a blue eye framed in dark lash

Hiding away in shadow far away

While the predator stalked his prey.

And the dark one looked out, amusedly

Placing sharp hungry knife in view

Pointed to its target, at my heart. Waiting.

The vodka poured and sloshed loudly

Against an expectant clear glass

And his teeth gleamed angry white

As he explained again the rules.

"You're going to die today, you know -

Unless you can win. You choose."

And my brain hops from fear into action

Analysing every situation in an instant

What can I give today,

To live through the night?

As my thought runs screaming through

A graveyard of failed ideas and hopes

He watches my expressions play out

And sits back with satisfaction gleaming

I sit with face frozen cold and listen

Smiling at his jokes and watching close

At his lounging demeanour like a cat

At his relaxed hands, not yet ready

To unleash blows on my body

The vodka flows again more freely

But not to me. This Game is not for me.

And the alcohol warms and frees him

And his rich laugh fills the room

I am winning, I think, I am living

And he turns so cold and looks in

The predator spies my hope so small

Growing in a secret part of my heart

And he says, so quiet - I haven't forgotten.

I'm still going to kill you.

And the Game continues on. I dance

With words and looks and silence

And watch the glass refill and knife shine

As I prepare to live another day if I win.

But the Game is ever against me.

If I win today then I lose tomorrow.

And the knife gleams expectantly

Holding its blood-lust tight within

It will always taste its prize again

If not today then always tomorrow.

And so the Game begins again.

Shadow Face

The fury quietly galvanises me

And I relish the chance to feel

As emotions run free and fast

But they run on a knife edge now.

My focus settles and sharpens

As my predatory self looks out

Carelessly taking over the reins

As I see your weaknesses gleaming

My joy rises furiously. And I smile.

The savage bloodlust appears

And I see the hurts that you hide

Trying to cover them so carefully.

I know now where to strike.

I do not see a human face now

With heart shining out bright

I see a collection of jumbled features

That I can take apart and break

Turning them under my heel.

Crushing them as you cry.

But I do not value hearts and tears

Surely I warned you of that?

I do not keep loyalty to the weak

Not when I leave behind my humanity

And cast off my stifling compassion
Now you have unleashed a creature
Who will not stop to mourn.
I burn my bridges with gaiety.
And if you step onto them, well.
I expect you will burn too.

Clarity

The deja vu resurfaces again
And I turn to it as an old friend
I had not missed its presence
Hovering at my elbow so silent
But now, on its timely return,
Its forethought reassures me.
I understand this.
This, I have lived before. Again.
And closely on her omnipotent heels
Come the clicks, a shudder of blink,
Blink and blink
As my brain fractures into a myriad
Of reflective pieces on the ground
And then they shiver and reform again.
The otherworldliness settles into place
And dissociation saunters back
Into his claimed corner again
Winking leisurely over his shoulder
As he claims his forgotten drink.
My world can be … restored.
And my brain adjusts quickly
To fit into these current quirks
The shudder, click, shudder

As my brain disconnects anew
And back, to a distorted reality
And the world struggles into
Its new, improved terrain
Of slightly unreal at the edges
And blurred clarity in the middle.
The numbness spreads slowly
Anaesthetic sewn in its cloak
And I welcome the cooling stain
As feeling retreats from me
And I can see.

Of Myth and Magic

Samhain

Samhain draws in, with the darker night

Can you hear the muffled sigh, the slowed

Tick of the clock, the veil pulling thinner?

Samhain is near, with the cooling breath

Of the dying God. The Lady stands still

Statuesque in grief - dark till Spring.

Can you feel the breath of your Ancestors?

The warm plate and a Dumb Supper

The creak of a door, a whisper of trees

The flicker of light before we step into the Dark

Time turns. The Year grows old. We begin again.

Sunset in a Cornfield

The sunlit corn sways and flows

Hearkening to a southerly wind

A thousand nodding heads dancing

In a rich yellow sea set in green

The sun shines down languidly

And she asks me now

What do you harvest here, child?

For Lammas approaches swiftly

Ushered in by a strong Buck Moon

And the promises of a heady summer

Await the word, to spill into our hands.

But what do I harvest here?

When I look out on the field of gold

I recall a thousand ancient summers

Of castles protected by noble Knight

Built swiftly with bales of hay and mirth

Sunburn and heat and rivers of hope

Dreams long gone into the winds

Yet the Sun faithfully gathered them

So lovingly to her fiery breast

And now, I ask myself

Which dreams do I open and fulfil?

To open them takes courage, you see

To make the dreams real, to live them

Instead of looking and sighing

And saying oh one day, maybe…

I will gather up my waiting corn

And hold it close, breathing in.

What do I harvest for Lammas?

I harvest all the joy, I say.

Mabon

Day and night draw into balance
A silence falls as the scale stills
The leaves fall and wither in fade
Colours evolve to orange and red
Green is left behind in old memory
Tomorrow the night will conquer
Drawing precious minutes away
From the slowly weakened Sun
The chill caresses my fingertips
And the autumn wind breathes
So gently, yet it calls my name
It is time to set away the warmth
And light a fire within our souls
To look now for our North Star
Our compass to hearken to
When all becomes dark and cold
Can you hear the quiet of Samhain
Leading her way in from the West
White bones gleaming starkly
Her touch quelling all brave life
She comes. She waits in the dark.
But first we mark the Equinox
The whispered hush of balance

Where our arms travel outwards
And pause as if they float in air
Light self and shadow self both
Standing in gentle opposition
And we wait for the inevitable
For the sun to fade in strength
And for the dark to creep in.

Samhain Eve

The strain of music notes spills out
Releasing memories bursting from the staves
The voices begin calling from beyond the grave
Reaching out for me, asking. Do you hear us?
The wind has stilled to a murmur now
The year has stalled as we wait together
The Goddess will fall endlessly in grief
And we will step out, out into the dark
As we did, and do and will again
Samhain calls us endlessly home.
But my ancestors await me in ancient memory
Asking me again if I will heed them.
What are we if we are merely the sum
Of what has gone before us?
Are we but an echo resonating through time?
Can we be more than a raindrop falling
And disappearing into an endless lake?
The past always calls me more potently
Than the present or even the future.
As we do not know what we cannot see
But our ancestors are carved so deep
Into our hands and our beating hearts
In our words and our songs and souls.

And the song reaching so soul deep

Conjures long forgotten memories

Of a car journey in the rain, and tears

Of mourning while I drove to see him

The man who was my father

To say farewell for the last time.

We cannot forget our ancestors who call

Father and Grandparents and departed friends

And on Samhain when the veil pulls thin

The melancholy pulls and turns me slow

And I hear them, I feel them touch my hand

And the grief of the loss reaches me anew.

Samhain is calling me. And she asks if I hear.

The Sea Dragons

If when we conjure dragons in our eye
We mean those of fire and flame
Crawling in caverns deep with gold
So carelessly claimed over paling bones
But what of the other dragon kinds
The kind who live quietly in the blue
Those who roam and reign in the wave
They, the ruthless rulers of the Sea?
Sea dragons there certainly were, and are
And ever indeed will there be
Cold amphibious wing trailing
Sweeping sinuously through the gleam
Shadow of smoke falling through the cold
And they turn and sneer and swim away
Perhaps untouched by cruel entropy
And an ever encroaching gravity
They were not forced to shrink and crawl
To unravel their jeweled armour fair
Growing limbs and losing their wing
Clutching at their vanishing dignity
No, the dragon Kings of the blue Sea
They kept their utter mastery, you see.
They reign over our wide oceans
In undiscovered depths and hollows

And mayhap they plan to rule the world

Just as they once did and will again

Forcing liege with watery claws sharp

And imposing dread with pale aqua eye

And holding anger in their hearts, at us

Who colonised here, next to them

Unknowingly, as they ruled the Seas

Perhaps when they rage in their wrath

They do not belch out withering flame

But instead they pull the fabric of the Sea

Each with a shimmering and sharp claw

Propelling their roof into a mountain of wrath

Unstoppable in its furious intensity.

The Sea Dragons still rule over us now

They may not fly to show their dominion

But they do imbue our small lives with fear

Creeping dark water and creatures that cling

Deadly bodies that can devour so coldly

As they sail past in a deadly deep Armada

Murderous torrential waves that climb

And crash and pillage and drown so cruel

Unstoppable in its fury and in its greed

They pull us down in turning sucking currents

Till we reach the bottom and replenish again

Their treasure, their underwater hoard.

In the Sea. There be Dragons.

Dragons in Myth

I see the dragons still, soaring in the sky

Their armoured skin gleaming in the glow

Their cold reptilian eye slowly blinking

Sharp taloned claw curving elegantly

And great wings spreading aloft in the sky

They say. Dragons are now but a myth

A story old that really should be forgot

Steeped in fairytale, ancient and primitive

That their flame no more blazes in the sky

But why are they so real, to me, I ask

If they are myth, why do they appear

Why do they live so, linger in our hearts

Why do our souls resonate in their tale?

I ponder my wish to fly far far away

Or high into the sky, skimming hills

And clipping great mountains with wing

My rage, burning hot and deep still

The flame of my words that destroy

Faces crumpling and melting in pain

Turning aside words weaponed cruel

With poisoned darts in angry flame

And my great wings stretch and thrash

So violently, huge jewelled wings

To keep good frightened people away

To keep them all at bay, far from me

And I wonder anew, in my heart

Are we the dragons in truth?

The dragons that were, that now

Sail in songs of myth and verse

Those great dragons of wing and flame

Who now will never fly high again?

And when I spy in clouds high aflame

Winged dragons flying high and free

I ask myself quietly. Do I actually see me?

Or me as was, my great ancestor now

Flying free in honour, courage and dignity

With wings of flame and sinew and bone

And a heart of strength and stern of face

Who flies so high among the clouds

Looping and curling in an aerial dance

Free to stretch her wings and fly

Strong and honourable and true

And here I am, crawling on this earth

But a distant and beggarly ancestor

Reaching out oh so expectantly

Trying to shrug off my choking cape

Of dark shame, my mundane self

Looking at those majestic dragons

Who fly and wheeling turn in the sky
Even when humans say they are myth
Yes myth they are, now, indeed
As they fly and lift and soar so freely.
I wish I was a dragon, I say wistfully.
You're a human, they say. Be grateful
For that. And I look and I sigh and I see.
I see them, the dragons of myth beyond.

Darkest Night

The stars are sighing

Embrace the dark

Honour your shadow

For standing at your back

Honour your loss

Look to the night

And let it fall ...

Tomorrow the light returns

The days stretch longer again...

Infinitesimally.

Take comfort in the pale Sun

And warm yourself by Brigid's flame

Honour your loss

And step forward once more.

Saint George and a Dragon

Light falls gently on an artful glass pane

Of a saint so brave, his sword in hand

And a slavering cowering beast, a dragon

Who must die in shame to Saint the Knight

Who then stands high in glory and pride

Taking the holy helm of a kingdom

And remains in glory, etched in glass

Gleaming darkly from the quiet cathedral

Inked in a window high above our heart.

But I do wonder still about the dragon.

Was he in truth feral and dangerous

And was he really a beast so dark?

Did he in truth harass and terrorise

Felling trees and scorching to bare earth

Ruthlessly stealing the helpless maid?

Did he deserve to be slain so cruelly

And pressed into a stained glass tableaux

Reds and gold scorching him eternally

Becoming the symbol of our own struggle

The dragon that we must also slay

I wish to set free the deposed dragon

And free it from its stained glass fetter

Maybe ask for its story, if it wish to tell

Of where it came from, of its dreams

And instead of killing the noble dragon

I would like to help find its freedom

To see it fly so high, great wings aloft

Sailing away far in the deep horizon

Leaving behind him a sneering Knight

His shining sword eternally aloft

Poised to slay his dreadful demons

That do not exist when you shine light

Through a fragment of stained glass.

Can They?

Can all beasts love nature, do you think?

From the small, crawling the earth

Nose to the ground, snuffling deep

To the flying predators gracefully cruel

Wheeling and swirling and dipping low

Do they love the world, the air they breathe?

Can a dragon love nature, do you think?

Or do they merely destroy and crush

Whipping destruction in dark fury

Plundering proud and burning wrath

Ripping the heart out of a plush green wood

Crushing trees and annihilating fauna

Then settling so sated in heart

On a smouldering throne of ash?

Perhaps if we found good fortune

We would espy a dragon proud

Tiptoe-ing through a quiet forest

Looking again at the shafts of light

And marvelling at the play of shadow

Or when he flies high in stately form

Over a mountain range jagged wide

And we would see their wing pause

As they gazed in rapturous awe

When the sun sets the peaks aflame?
Perhaps as they wander in dream
They see and hear in colour warm
And hear sound so rich and clear
Singing fountains in mountain springs
And gurgling streams on golden sand
And smell the intoxicating fragrance
Of ancient tall cedar trees reaching up
And hearken sweetly to the orchestra
Of birds in a staggered harmony
And perhaps as they dream of this
They sigh and smile. They are home.

The North Wind

I call the North Wind

I call the corners with intention

Turning through the compass

Feeling the sand under my feet

And the cool breath expectant

Whispering through my hair

And I step to the regal North

I look into the rolling grey Wind

A deep fog swirls in sharp cold

This is the centre of the earth

The clear night, holding so still

I see you, O North Wind

Black of heart and night

And cold as bitter death

I see your fingers reaching

To freeze my fear away

A dark figure walking slow

Across the grey silver sand

I feel you, O North Wind

And your cold abrasive might

Stripping me of my regret

Ripping back my defenses

Dissolving them into mist

And I stand without shield
But I do not quake at your face
So dark and still and strange
You walk in the dead of night
With the unseen at your side
But you are the one who
Fiercely holds us still
Who clears our blinded eyes
Who rips away our tears
And grounds us to the Earth
I call the corners with love
Knowing now who you are
A solemn and silent guide
Yet a cold and remote storm
Flowing through our dark.
I bid you hail and welcome
O dark Wind of the North.
I see you. For we are kin.

The East Wind

As the compass shifts again
And I turn slowly to the East
Time twisting along with me
And I look to meet the Wind

The sky lightens sweetly
As a new sunrise beckons
And the air lifts so gently
In a new and joyous morn

The East Wind is capricious
Fierce in his hunger for storm
And rampaging in spring gusts
As he asserts his dominance
Over all that stands in his way

O East Wind I do see you
Smiling in your capricity
One moment beckoning
And drawing me to you
In inexorable dance

And the next you turn
Cold face set in desertion
I smell the warm sunlit sand
And the damp dancing leaves
And the sated fat raindrops

That are waiting to fall

On me - so very ruthlessly.

In early spring I stand now

Waiting for you to dance

And you clasp my hand

To whirl me in a frenzy

Of exhilarating speed

And then to tumble, slow

In a dizzying collapse

And the white blooms settle

Around my sodden feet.

You are an enigma, O East Wind

Charm divine but

Dark in destructive rage

Inconstant and vain,

Yet radiant in sunrise

The Spring's Gallant.

I return to the corners

And bow deep to you

O shining East Wind

As I call the corners anew

No constant friend are you

But an occasional dancer

And a memory of spring

I bid you hail and welcome

And namaste, for we are kin.

The South Wind

As the wheel turns slowly

And spring bows to summer

And I greet the South Corner

Warmly with smiles of intent

As I greet an amiable friend

I look into her golden face

Warm and rich and strong

I hear the song of harvest

And the weighty vow of Jera

That the day is deep and long

And I close my eyes slowly

This is where I belong

I see you, O South Wind

With hollow ruddied cheeks

Like ripe russet apples

Holding warm summer rain

That sings an ancient melody

Of life and breeze and love

I feel you, O South Wind

And your calming breeze

As we sit down together

Oh so peaceably

The leaves dance around us

In harmonious chorus

And the bees join the hum

Summer waits in your arms

I have always known you

The wind of my summer

You greeted me as I grew

With spirited laugh of Lammas

You are an old friend to me

Mirthful, sweet and warm

The Fair Lady of the Sun.

As I call again the corners

I sing to you, the South

My dear, dear friend

Of fire and storm and dreams

I bid you hail and welcome

And I salute you. For we are kin.

The West Wind

The last corner awaits me

Dreaming in autumn dusk

That moment fleeting between

Day surrendering to night

The dusk draws a cool breath

And the sky pales and stills

And I turn slowly, to see Her

Standing in starlit pearl grey

The Lady of the West Wind.

She turns and sees me waiting

And smiles softly in welcome

Beckoning with open hand

For me to follow behind

The leaves rustle, falling gently

As we disappear into the grey

And silence envelops me

As if the earth has drawn breath

That will never be released

Again.

Expectantly I sit in the quiet

Waiting for Her to speak

Will I hear you, O West Wind?

What guidance do you bring

Within your calming wings?

What can your water tell me?

Can I find healing now, here

Among the slumbering trees

And the gently humming breeze?

But she merely looks, and smiles

And touches my face gently

And her voice chimes in my heart

Like the clustering evening birds

Gathered at silvered waterfalls.

"The healing lies in you alone

O young supplicant of Air

I hold the answers that you seek

And I wash away your wounds

But my healing sings best

In the silence, and pull of twilight

And the soft smell of evening rain.

In the quiet, you will ever find me."

I bow low to you, O West Wind

And your translucent face smiles

In slight tremor of soft breeze

And with sweep of drying leaves

Your silvered gown bending

You turn gently to move away

I call the corners softly to you

Knowing now who you are
And I sing to you, West Wind
As I complete the circle of day
And offer my love, as we are kin.

Fire

The fire crackles and calls me
As the day pools into night
Swirling staggered in a circle
Crouching on a deserted beach
And surrounded by white rock walls.
It burns so quietly while it waits
And it waits for me.
I must begin my journey.
I approach, raising my palms
And the sparks lift and dance
In happy recognition of fire
Meeting fire, as like sees like
A reflection of kindred souls.
The fire does not warm me
But it draws me deep within
The cold searing exploding
And I see great hot sparks
Descending, knowing deep
Fire holds ancient memory.
The fire never capitulates
It swallows its foes whole
Claiming their feared dread
And shallow plaintive scream

It remembers devouring deep

Burning, breaking, pillaging

Glorying yet still in its gluttony.

The crackle draws my eye

And I am swept away again

This time on a voyage through

Tall ancient castles and wide seas

Great empires rising and falling

And now shivering in the flames.

Fire is an ancient storyteller.

It will not keep your secrets.

The flames dance sinuously

With creeping reaching arms

The blaze widens and falls

Hypnotising me slowly

As I stand so transfixed

Fire anaesthetises swiftly

Cauterising our taut scars

Smoothing over sharp edges

And shining skin like pearls

But the process brings change

And you will never return

From your journeying.

Know this well,

O Daughters of flame.

My eyes burn and sting

As the water in my soul

Vanishes in stark flame

The soft heart within

Is burned and singed away

Slumping into feathered ash.

But the flame continues

In its endless dance of song

Fire. What secrets do you hold?

What do you have in store for me?

What must I yet learn?

I yearn to step within the flame

And bend it to my iron will

Subsumed with blazing spark

To know the ancient songs

To sing within their melody

But fire smiles and dances

With crackle of wood and spark

And I return to a cool beach

With night creeping around

And I wonder, again and anew

Fire. Who are you really?

Selkie

The sun warms my skin

And the sea calls my name

But I still sit and wait

So anxiously

To see if She will come again.

Sometimes at dusk she walks

Upon the silvery salt sand

A soft wind blowing strands of hair

Like the ghost of a mother's caress

And she looks out searchingly to sea

As if she is searching for me.

My hands reach out to touch her

And frame her perfect face

I long to call her and speak her name

The name I sang so softly into her skin

This human baby that my body bore

He captured me and kept my skin

My beloved seal shape in shadow

And I staggered on land hopelessly

Until She came and made me whole

For a blessed time

But the Sea ever called me Home

So insistently it jangled in my ear

I ached to regain my proper form

And swim with fur and warmth

I needed salt on my skin

And the embrace of my sisters

So I kissed my child and slipped away

To the dark grey sea to be free

But my heart still returns to the shore.

To look for Her and to silently call

To see her walk on the sand in dusk

Tall and lithe like a silver tree

And my heart breaks and sings

For my motherless child, who I love

But a mother I cannot be

For I still belong to the Sea.

aze

Green tendrils rising high into the sky

Almost forbidding in its great scale

The entrance looms ahead. Waiting.

There is only one way in. One way out.

What lies within those evergreen walls?

Each crossroads a tantalising thought

A possibility of a different potential life

And all you have to do is turn left or right.

Just choose.

So which road do you seek this time?

Temptation beckons quiet, to peek ahead

A surreptitious flicking ahead of pages

Just to see if this path is a dead end

Or if maybe it is actually the right way.

But I have no scarlet thread of old

And no divine hand at my shoulder

Guiding me with otherworldly intent

I have no clear white lantern of gift

With which I can light my way home.

So I must go on steady into the dark

Into the maze, pushing on forward

And face myself in fractured relief

As a million possibilities push forth

Different directions spark out infinitely

As I reach endlessly, hopelessly now

For the coveted centre. For my North Star.

But yet for myself. For the start and the End.

The Raven Call

The grey wind sings slowly

And the dark ravens call

The crossroads are barren

And so quiet now, waiting

Merely an intake of breath.

Looking from left to right

I see roads that stretch out

But they appear the same.

The undulations are there

They hold the same Fate.

If each road ends as the same

Then perhaps you cannot escape

What they say is your Fate.

But what if I choose not to play?

So I set down the cursed dice

Gently on the expectant ground.

I choose not to choose my road.

I choose not to make the same mistake

I choose not to play this doomed hand

I choose to at last walk away.

And the ravens call me back as I leave

I close my eyes to what they say

That this is my true destiny

But dark face wise in feather
Cannot define for me my road
They see not what my eyes see
They hear not what my heart hears
They feel not what my tears feel.
I will not heed the Raven's call
I will not throw the graveyard dice
I will not choose at the crossroads
I will not play this hand.
I throw it all up gently into the air
Watching it float up endlessly
And I turn not needing to see the fall
As I choose my own road to walk
And the sun slowly starts to rise.

Acknowledgements

There are many I need to thank for this poetry book, not least the people who I have shamelessly been inspired by, be they anonymous people in the street, the overheard conversations, artists who have made songs that I played endlessly on repeat while I wrote myself into a frenzy; or friends who cheerleaded me, inspired me and read my poetry. I particularly want to thank Katie, Tom, David and Lis for always telling me when a poem touched their soul. I want to thank the person who tirelessly read all my poems and pointed out when our conversations became imagery. To my favourite tsunami, thank you for being you.

About the Poet

Eryn McConnell

Eryn was born and raised in Oxford, UK, but nowadays lives in South Germany with their young family. They have a great dream to travel and visit all the great mountains and lakes of the world. They are a qualified History and English teacher, working freelance with international students.

They have been writing poetry since she was sixteen, including Middle-Earth fan poetry that has appeared in the Tolkien Society's publication, *Amon Hen*, and appearing in a music anthology for Sweetycat Press.

In addition to writing poetry they study with the Order of Bards, Ovates and Druids to be a druid, and they are working on a fantasy series which appears to involve steampunk, sky pirates, astral travel and lots of dragons.

If you want to see more of her writing, you can find her on

Facebook @ErynMcConnell.Writer

and Instagram @erynmcconnellwriter

Printed in Great Britain
by Amazon

86515243R00072